FORD POWELL

Idaho Adventures

50 Adventures that are not National Parks (plus a few bonuses)

Contents

Introduction

Welcome to Idaho Adventures – Beyond the Beaten Path

Idaho, known as the Gem State, offers a stunning array of landscapes and activities that cater to diverse interests and preferences. Idaho's natural beauty provides the perfect back-drop for various outdoor adventures and experiences, from rugged mountains and dense forests to serene lakes and vast deserts. Idaho's diverse landscapes and abundant recreational opportunities make it a paradise for outdoor enthusiasts and nature lovers. Whether you're seeking adrenaline-pumping adventures or peaceful retreats in nature, Idaho has something to offer everyone.

In a world where the grandeur of Yellowstone, the majesty of the Grand Canyon, and the serenity of Yosemite often dominate our conversations about nature, many lesser-known wonders are waiting to be discovered. We will explore some of these hidden gems in Idaho that offer unique adventures that rival even the most famous national parks. This book is an invitation to journey beyond the beaten path, to explore the extraordinary in the seemingly ordinary, and to find magic in places where relatively few have ventured. Each destination holds its own story and allure.

But this book is not just about discovering new places; it is about experiencing them in ways that challenge our perceptions and deepen our connection with the natural world. Whether you are an intrepid explorer seeking the thrill of the unknown, a nature enthusiast yearning for tranquility and solitude, or a curious wanderer looking to expand your horizons, you will find inspiration and guidance within these pages. So, pack your curiosity and prepare to embark on a journey that transcends the ordinary.

This book is organized into five parts:

1) Outdoor Excursions (Chapters 1-5)

2) Scenic Drives and Road Trips (Chapters 6-9)

3) Unique Attractions and Hidden Gems (Chapters 10-13)

4) Adventure Activities (Chapters 14-16)

5) Family-Friendly Adventures (Chapters 17-19)

Chapter 1: Hiking Trails

1 - Alpine Lake Trail

The Alpine Lake Trail (44°03′53″N 115°01′21″W) is nestled within the stunning Sawtooth Wilderness of Idaho. This scenic gem is renowned for its breathtaking landscapes and rugged beauty. This trail offers outdoor enthusiasts an immersive experience in one of Idaho's most pristine natural environments, showcasing the dramatic peaks, clear alpine waters, and diverse flora and fauna of the Sawtooth Wilderness. The trail is a moderately challenging hike that stretches approximately 12 miles round-trip. It starts at the Iron Creek Trailhead, accessible from Stanley. The trail gradually ascends through lush pine and fir forests.

One of the highlights of the Alpine Lake Trail is its namesake, Alpine Lake, a serene and picturesque destination in a high basin surrounded by steep granite cliffs. The lake's crystal-clear waters reflect the surrounding peaks, creating a postcard-worthy scene that is particularly stunning during the early morning or late afternoon when the light is soft. The Alpine Lake Trail is best hiked from late June through early October. Early in the season, snow can linger on higher sections of the trail, making conditions challenging. Summer and early fall offer the most reliable weather and trail conditions, though afternoon thunderstorms can occur.

Alpine Lake

2 - Window Arch Trail

The Window Arch Trail (42°04′12″N 113°42′45″W) is located in the City of Rocks National Reserve, an area with striking granite rock formations and scenic vistas. Hikers can experience unique geological features that make the City of Rocks a popular destination. The Window Arch Trail is a moderately challenging hike that leads to the Window Arch, a natural rock arch formation that resembles a window. The trail is relatively short, making it accessible for many hikers, including families and those not looking for an all-day trek. The hike typically takes about 1 to

1.5 hours to complete the round trip, depending on the pace and time spent exploring the arch and its surroundings.

The Window Arch Trail trailhead is easily accessible from the main roads within the City of Rocks National Reserve. Ample parking is available at the trailhead, and informational signs provide details about the trail and the area's natural history. The trail begins with a gentle ascent through a landscape dotted with large boulders and native vegetation. As you progress, the path becomes steeper and more rugged, requiring careful footing over rocky terrain. Along the way, hikers are treated to panoramic views of the surrounding valleys and rock formations. The hike's highlight is, of course, the Window Arch itself. This impressive natural feature is a testament to the erosive forces of wind and water that have shaped the region over millions of years. The arch frames views of the landscape beyond, creating a picturesque scene.

Window Arch

3 - Snake River Trail

The Snake River Trail (45°22′17″N 116°38′18″W) is located in Hells Canyon. It is a stunning and challenging hiking trail that allows adventurers to explore one of North America's deepest river gorges. Hells Canyon, carved by the Snake River, forms a natural border between Idaho and Oregon and is renowned for its dramatic landscapes and diverse wildlife. The Snake River Trail is a 27-mile long (one-way), rugged path that stretches along the Idaho side of the Snake River within Hells Canyon National Recreation Area. The trail offers hikers a combination of breathtaking scenery, historical sites, and opportunities for wildlife viewing.

Hells Canyon

The trail provides continuous views of the Snake River and the towering canyon walls. The scenery is especially striking during sunrise and sunset when the light accentuates the textures and colors of the landscape. The trail passes several historical sites, including old homesteads, mining relics, and Native American petroglyphs. The best seasons for hiking the Snake River Trail are spring and fall, with moderate temperatures and more predictable weather. Summer can be sweltering, with temperatures often exceeding 100°F. There are several designated campsites along the trail. These sites offer basic amenities like fire rings and flat areas for tents. Some sites also provide access to fresh water sources.

Chapter 2: Water Adventures

4 - Payette River Rafting

Whitewater rafting on the Payette River (44°05′32″N 116°57′09″W) offers an exhilarating adventure through picturesque land-scapes. The river is renowned for its thrilling rapids, diverse rafting routes, and stunning natural scenery, making it a prime destination for novice and experienced rafters. The North Fork of the Payette River, known for its challenging Class IV and V rapids, is ideal for experienced rafters seeking a high-adrenaline adventure. Rapids like "Jacob's Ladder" and "Congo" test even the most seasoned rafters with their powerful currents and steep drops. The main Payette River is more accessible to intermediate rafters, featuring Class II to III rapids. It offers a good blend of excitement and safety, making it popular for families and those looking to enjoy a thrilling yet manageable ride. Key rapids include "Mike's Hole" and "Mixmaster." The South Fork of the Payette River offers a mix of moderate to challenging Class III to IV rapids. This section includes famous rapids such as "Staircase" and "Slalom." The South Fork is well-loved for its dynamic rapids and scenic views, which include rugged canyons and forested landscapes.

The rafting season on the Payette River typically runs from late spring to early fall, with water levels peaking in late spring and early summer due to snowmelt. As the season progresses, the water levels decrease, making the rapids slightly less intense but enjoyable. The best time to go depends on the type of experience desired – higher, faster water early in the season or slightly milder conditions later.

Payette River

5 - Kayaking Below Shoshone Falls

Shoshone Falls (42°35′43″N 114°24′03″W), often referred to as the "Niagara of the West," is located on the Snake River near Twin Falls. At 212 feet, it surpasses Niagara Falls and creates a powerful spectacle of cascading water, particularly during spring when the river's flow peaks due to snowmelt. Kayaking below Shoshone Falls in Idaho offers an exhilarating and unique experience for paddlers, combining the thrill of navigating challenging rapids with the awe-inspiring beauty of one of the most iconic waterfalls in the United States.

Shoshone Falls

Kayaking below Shoshone Falls is not for the faint of heart. The area is known for its intense rapids and challenging water conditions, making it more suitable for experienced kayakers. The water flow can vary significantly depending on the time of year and river management practices, influencing the difficulty of the rapids. To kayak below Shoshone Falls, paddlers typically launch from below the dam or at designated access points along the Snake River. It is crucial to check local regulations and water conditions beforehand, as water released from the dam can affect river levels and safety. The journey downstream offers stunning views of the rugged canyon walls, lush vegetation, and wildlife. The mighty roar of the falls serves as a constant back-drop, adding to the adventure's dramatic ambiance. Paddlers may also encounter serene stretches of river between the rapids, providing opportunities to take in the natural surroundings and perhaps even spot local wildlife such as ospreys, herons, and river otters.

6 - Stand-Up Paddleboarding at Priest Lake

Priest Lake (48°34′N 116°52′W) is renowned for its crystal-clear waters, which are fed by mountain streams and surrounded by lush forests. The lake spans over 19 miles and offers breathtak-ing views of the Selkirk Mountains. Paddlers can enjoy serene, glassy waters, especially in the early mornings or late evenings when the lake is calm and peaceful. Standup paddleboarding (SUP) at Priest Lake in Idaho offers a fantastic way to experience the area's pristine beauty. Known as the "Crown Jewel" of North Idaho, Priest Lake is a stunning location for paddleboarding.

The lake's extensive shoreline and numerous bays, inlets, and islands provide endless opportunities for exploration. You can paddle to the secluded Upper Priest Lake, accessible via a narrow, 2.5-mile-long waterway known as the Thorofare. This area is remarkably tranquil and offers an authentic wilderness experience, as it's only accessible by boat or on foot. The area is home to diverse wildlife, including bald eagles, ospreys, deer, and occasionally moose. In addition to paddleboarding, the lake is ideal for swimming, kayaking, and fishing.

Priest Lake

BONUS #1: Redfish Lake

Redfish Lake (44°7′N 114°56′W) is a stunning alpine lake located in the Sawtooth National Recreation Area near Stanley. It is renowned for its clear blue waters and breathtaking mountain scenery, making it a popular destination for outdoor enthusiasts and nature lovers. Redfish Lake is situated at an elevation of approximately 6,550 feet (1,996 meters) in the Sawtooth Valley. It is about 4.5 miles (7.2 kilometers) long and 0.72 miles (1.2 kilometers) wide, covering an area of around 1,518 acres. The lake is fed by glacial runoff and mountain streams, contributing to its pristine water quality.

Redfish Lake

The lake gets its name from the sockeye salmon, known as "redfish" due to their vibrant red color during spawning. Historically, many sockeye salmon migrated from the Pacific Ocean to Redfish Lake to spawn, traveling over 900 miles. The area surrounding Redfish Lake has been used by Native American tribes for thousands of years, primarily for fishing and hunting. The lake offers excellent opportunities for boating, with several boat ramps and marinas available. Fishing is also popular, with species like rainbow trout, kokanee salmon, and bull trout in the lake. Numerous hiking trails originate from the lake, leading into the Sawtooth Wilderness. Campgrounds and lodges around the lake provide various accommodation options for visitors.

Chapter 3: Mountain Biking

7 - Ridge to Rivers Trail System

The Ridge to Rivers Trail System (43°36′57″N 116°12′6″W) is a multi-use network in the foothills surrounding Boise. Spanning over 190 miles, this extensive trail system is a vital recreational resource for residents and visitors, offering various trails suitable for hiking, mountain biking, and horseback riding. The trail system features single-track trails, dirt roads, and paved paths, providing options for all skill levels and activities.

The Table Rock Trail is a challenging hike that rewards trekkers with panoramic views of Boise and the surrounding area from the iconic Table Rock plateau. Hull's Gulch Reserve offers trails like the Lower Hulls Gulch Trail, known for its lush vegetation and scenic beauty. Camel's Back Park is a family-friendly area with easy access to trails that meander through the foothills and provide stunning vistas.

Boise

8 - Jug Mountain Ranch Trails

The Jug Mountain Ranch Trail System is an extensive trail system near McCall that offers various recreational opportunities across its diverse terrain. The trail network at Jug Mountain Ranch is comprehensive, providing options for all skill levels. Whether you're a beginner looking for a stroll through meadows and forests or an experienced mountain biker seeking challenging climbs and thrilling descents, the trails are designed to cater to a wide range of abilities. The trails are meticulously maintained and well-marked, ensuring a safe and enjoyable experience for all visitors.

Jug Bay Wetlands

The Jug Mountain Loop Trail offers panoramic views of the surrounding mountains and valleys, providing a moderately challenging hike with rewarding vistas. The Lake Trail is a scenic route that takes you to the serene Jug Mountain Lake, perfect for a peaceful nature walk or a picnic by the water. Jug Mountain Ranch is particularly renowned for its mountain biking trails. With a dedicated trail crew, the ranch offers some of the best single-track riding in Idaho. Berm N' Ernie is known for its flowy berms and fun jumps; this trail is a favorite among thrill-seekers. Doe Joe is a challenging trail featuring technical sections and rocky terrain, ideal for advanced riders looking to test their skills. The South Boundary Trail is a longer ride that offers a mix of technical challenges and breathtaking views, perfect for those seeking an adventurous day out.

9 - Discovery Hill Trails

The Discovery Hill Trails near Salmon include over 30 miles of trails that cater to different skill levels and activities. The trails weave through rolling hills, dense forests, and open meadows, providing users with various enjoyable environments. The area is well-marked with signs and maps at trailheads, ensuring visitors can easily navigate the network. The trails vary in difficulty, from gentle, family-friendly paths to more challenging routes for seasoned hikers and mountain bikers.

Nestled in the Salmon-Challis National Forest, this trail system provides outdoor enthusiasts with various terrains and breathtaking views of the surrounding landscapes. Discovery Hill Loop is a moderate loop trail offering a mix of smooth sections and rocky patches, making it suitable for intermediate hikers and bikers. Stinky Springs Trail features a mix of climbs and descents through diverse landscapes. North Ridge Trail is a challenging route with steep climbs and technical sections, perfect for advanced mountain bikers.

Discovery Hills Trail

Chapter 4: Rock Climbing

10 – Rock Climbing at Castle Rocks

Castle Rocks State Park (42°07′33″N 113°39′32″W) is a premier rock-climbing destination, offering a range of climbing experiences amidst stunning natural scenery. Located near Almo and adjacent to the more well-known City of Rocks National Reserve, Castle Rocks is known for its unique geological formations, providing various climbing challenges for all skill levels. The park is characterized by its granite spires, domes, and boulders, which have been sculpted by wind, water, and time into distinctive shapes. These features offer numerous climbing routes, ranging from beginner-friendly slabs to challenging overhangs and cracks. The granite here is renowned for its high quality, providing excellent friction and solid holds.

Popular climbing areas include The Castle, which has traditional and sport climbing routes. Its towering spires and walls provide challenging climbs with breathtaking views of the surrounding landscape. The Lower Breadloaves is ideal for beginners and those looking for less intimidating climbs. The routes here are well-bolted and provide an excellent introduction to the rock quality and style found in the park. The Upper

Breadloaves is suited for climbers looking to push their limits. The climbs here are steeper and more technical, requiring a higher level of skill and experience.

Castle Rocks

11 – Bouldering in Massacre Rocks State Park

Massacre Rocks State Park (42°40'39"N 112°59'11"W) near American Falls on the Snake River is renowned for its rich history, dramatic landscapes, and excellent bouldering opportunities. Bouldering at Massacre Rocks offers a unique experience due to the area's volcanic geology, which has created a vast array of rocks and formations ideal for climbers of various skill levels. Massacre Rocks is a product of ancient volcanic activity, with the Snake River Plain providing a backdrop of basalt and rhyolite formations. These volcanic rocks have weathered over millennia, creating diverse boulders with varying shapes, sizes, and textures. The unique formations result from natural weathering and the ancient Bonneville Flood, which sculpted the landscape thousands of years ago.

Massacre Rocks boasts a wide range of bouldering problems, making it suitable for climbers of all abilities. The area features everything from beginner-friendly slabs and low-angle faces to more challenging overhangs. Climbers at Massacre Rocks are treated to stunning views of the Snake River and the surrounding high desert landscape. The park's natural beauty, rugged terrain, rich flora, and fauna enhance the overall climbing experience. The serene environment also offers a peaceful escape, making it a popular spot for bouldering and relaxation.

Massacre Rocks

12 - Climbing the Black Cliffs

Climbing the Black Cliffs is a popular activity for outdoor enthusiasts, offering a unique and challenging experience for climbers of various skill levels. Located just a short drive from downtown Boise along Highway 21, these basalt cliffs provide a stunning backdrop and a variety of climbing routes. The Black Cliffs are composed primarily of basalt, a volcanic rock that forms from the rapid cooling of basaltic lava. The cliffs were created by volcanic activity millions of years ago, resulting in the striking, dark-colored rock formations that give them their name. The vertical and columnar basalt formations offer a unique and visually impressive climbing environment, with the Boise River flowing nearby, adding to the scenic beauty.

Black Cliffs

The Black Cliffs are renowned for their wide range of climbing routes, catering to beginners and experienced climbers. The routes vary in difficulty, from easier climbs suitable for novice climbers to more challenging routes that test the skills of seasoned climbers. The Sunset Area is perfect for beginners and those looking to warm up. The North Central Area offers a mix of moderate to challenging climbs, attracting intermediate climbers. The Asylum features some of the most difficult routes, with overhangs and technical climbs for advanced climbers. The cliffs are primarily used for sport climbing, with many routes equipped with bolts and anchors. However, there are also opportunities for traditional climbing and bouldering.

Chapter 5: Winter Sports

13 – Cross-Country Skiing in Sun Valley

Sun Valley (43°40′50″N 114°20′34″W) is a premier destination for cross-country skiing, offering a unique combination of beautiful scenery, well-maintained trails, and a rich history in winter sports. Sun Valley boasts an extensive network of over 125 miles of groomed Nordic trails, catering to all skill levels. The trails are meticulously maintained, ensuring a smooth and enjoyable experience. The varied terrain includes everything from flat, easy tracks perfect for beginners to more challenging, hilly courses for experienced skiers. Skiers glide through serene pine forests, open meadows, and frozen rivers, all set against the backdrop of the majestic Boulder and Sawtooth Mountains.

Sun Valley

Sun Valley Nordic & Snowshoe Center offers access to various trails and provides amenities like equipment rentals, lessons, and a comfortable lodge for après-ski relaxation. Galena Lodge and Trails provides a more rustic and serene environment and is a favorite for its scenic trails, backcountry options, and charming lodge. Harriman Trail runs along the Big Wood River, connecting the Sawtooth National Recreation Area to the Blaine County Recreation District trails.

14 - Snowmobiling at Brundage Mountain

Brundage Mountain (45.005°N 116.155°W) offers an exhilarating and scenic experience for winter sports enthusiasts. Located in the heart of the Payette National Forest, it is renowned for its deep powder and diverse terrain, making it a prime destination for snowmobiling. Brundage Mountain boasts over 320 miles of groomed snowmobile trails, ranging from beginner-friendly routes to challenging backcountry adventures. The trails weave through dense forests, open meadows, and along ridgelines, providing riders with stunning views of the surrounding mountains and valleys. The elevation reaches up to 7,640 feet, ensuring consistent snowfall and excellent riding conditions throughout winter.

One of the highlights of snowmobiling at Brundage Mountain is the opportunity to witness the breathtaking winter landscape. The snow-covered trees, frozen lakes, and panoramic mountain views create a picturesque setting. Wildlife sightings are common, with animals like elk, deer, and bird species often spotted along the trails.

Brundage Mountain

15 – Snowshoeing at Ponderosa State Park

Ponderosa State Park (44°55'40"N, 116°04'56"W) offers a winter wonderland perfect for snowshoeing enthusiasts. Located near McCall, this state park is known for its stunning landscapes, diverse wildlife, and extensive network of trails catering to outdoor adventurers of all skill levels. Ponderosa State Park spans over 1,500 acres on a peninsula that juts into Payette Lake. The park is named after the towering ponderosa pines that dominate its forests, creating a picturesque backdrop for winter activities. Snowshoeing through the park immerses visitors in a serene environment, surrounded by snow-covered trees,

27

frosted meadows, and breathtaking views.

Ponderosa State Park boasts a variety of trails that are ideal for snowshoeing. These trails range from accessible, beginner-friendly routes to more challenging paths. Meadow Marsh Trail offers a relatively easy and flat route through the park's scenic meadows and marshlands. Fox Run Trail is a moderate trail that winds through dense forests and open clearings, providing ample opportunities for wildlife spotting and enjoying the park's tranquil beauty. Ridgeline Trail offers a steeper climb with rewarding views of Payette Lake and the surrounding mountains. Beyond snowshoeing, Ponderosa State Park is a hub for various winter activities. Cross-country skiing is popular, with many of the park's trails groomed for skiing. The park also offers opportunities for ice fishing on Payette Lake and has designated areas for sledding.

Ponderosa State Park

BONUS #2: Kelly Canyon Resort

Kelly Canyon Resort (43°38′45″N 111°37′48″W) is a well-loved destination for outdoor enthusiasts, offering a blend of activities that cater to both winter and summer adventures. Located near Ririe, this resort is known for its family-friendly atmosphere, diverse terrain, and year-round recreational opportunities. During winter, Kelly Canyon Resort becomes a haven for skiers and snowboarders. The resort features over 640 acres of skiable terrain with various runs suitable for all skill levels, from beginner to expert. The elevation at the summit reaches approximately 6,600 feet, providing ample snow coverage and breathtaking views of the surrounding mountains. One of the unique features of Kelly Canyon is its night skiing offerings. With well-lit trails, visitors can extend their skiing and snowboarding experiences into the evening, enjoying Idaho's crisp, clear night skies. The resort offers snowshoeing and Nordic skiing trails for those who prefer a slower pace. These trails wind through serene, snow-covered forests, providing a peaceful and scenic alternative to downhill skiing.

When the snow melts, Kelly Canyon Resort becomes a premier destination for mountain biking. The resort offers a network of trails that vary in difficulty, catering to novice and experienced riders. The trails are well-maintained and take advantage of the natural terrain, featuring thrilling descents and challenging climbs. Hiking is another popular summer activity at Kelly Canyon. The resort's trails offer a range of experiences, from easy walks to more strenuous hikes. The trails meander through lush forests and open meadows and offer stunning views of the surrounding landscape. Kelly Canyon also features a disc golf course, providing visitors with a fun and challenging activity.

The course is set against the backdrop of the scenic mountain terrain, adding an extra layer of enjoyment to the game.

Chapter 6: Panhandle Prowl

16 – US Route 95: Coeur d'Alene to Sandpoint

Driving from Coeur d'Alene (47°41′34″N 116°46′48″W) to Sandpoint (48°16′N 116°34′W) along U.S. Route 95 is a scenic 47-mile journey through Northern Idaho, offering a mix of picturesque landscapes, small-town charm, and natural beauty. The route starts on the north shore of Lake Coeur d'Alene and follows U.S. Route 95 north to Sandpoint, with the drive taking approximately one hour, depending on traffic and weather. The highway starts as a multi-lane road with commercial areas, gradually transitioning to more rural and scenic landscapes.

The drive passes through Dalton Gardens and Hayden near Hayden Lake, then to Rathdrum Prairie. This open, flat area provides views of surrounding mountains and agricultural fields. The route continues north through Athol, home of Silverwood Theme Park, the largest theme park in the Pacific Northwest. Consider a stop at Silverwood if you have time for roller coasters and water rides. Farragut State Park, located east of U.S. Route 95, provides hiking, boating, and wildlife viewing opportunities. One of the highlights of the drive is the Long Bridge, which spans the Pend Oreille River as it flows out of Lake Pend Oreille and provides an approach to Sandpoint.

Highway 95, Lake Pend Oreille

17 - Schweitzer Mountain

Schweitzer Mountain Resort (48.367°N 116.623°W) is a premier ski destination in the Selkirk Mountains near Sandpoint. Known for its stunning views, diverse terrain, and welcoming atmosphere, Schweitzer offers a variety of activities for visitors year-round. The resort boasts over 2,900 acres of skiable terrain, with 92 designated trails. The terrain is well-suited for all skill levels, from beginner slopes to advanced runs. Schweitzer also features two open bowls, the South Bowl and the Outback Bowl, providing excellent powder skiing and snowboarding opportunities. Additionally, the resort has a terrain park for freestyle enthusiasts and extensive Nordic skiing trails for cross-country skiers.

Top of Schweitzer Mountain

In the summer, Schweitzer transforms into an outdoor recreation hub. Visitors can enjoy mountain biking, hiking, and scenic chairlift rides. The resort's mountain bike park offers trails ranging from beginner to advanced, making it a popular spot for riders. Hiking trails provide access to stunning vistas and the opportunity to explore the rich natural beauty of the

Selkirk Mountains. Schweitzer also hosts events like music festivals, outdoor yoga, and family-friendly activities during the summer months.

Chapter 7: Lewis and Clark Trail

18 - U.S. Highway 12: Lolo Pass to Lewiston

Driving from Lolo Pass (46.635°N 114.580°W), elevation 5,233 feet, to Lewiston (46.41°N 117.02°W) along U.S. Highway 12 is a scenic and historically significant journey that traverses some of the most beautiful and rugged landscapes in the Pacific Northwest. This route follows the path of the historic Lewis and Clark Expedition. It offers travelers a mix of breathtaking scenery, outdoor recreational opportunities, and glimpses into the region's rich cultural heritage. The Lolo Pass Visitor Center provides historical exhibits, maps, and information about the area's natural and cultural history.

From Lolo Pass, the route follows U.S. Highway 12, also known as the Northwest Passage Scenic Byway to Lewiston. The total distance of 150 miles can be driven in about 3 to 4 hours without stops. However, the journey is best enjoyed leisurely, allowing time for sightseeing, hiking, and exploring the numerous points of interest. Lolo Hot Springs offers a relaxing stop with natural hot springs pools, a restaurant, and lodging options. Clearwater National Forest provides hiking, fishing, and camping opportunities. The Lochsa River is renowned for its white-water rafting and fishing opportunities. Heart of the Monster features a unique rock formation central to the Nez Perce creation story. In Orofino, Canoe Camp marks the site where the Lewis and Clark Expedition built canoes to continue their journey down the Clearwater River.

Lolo Pass

19 - Clearwater River Historic Sites

The Clearwater River is a historically rich region with numerous significant sites reflecting the cultural and historical heritage of the area. Kamiah (46°13′37″N 116°1′40″W) is one of the oldest settlements in the region, with deep roots in Nez Perce history. The town is home to the Nez Perce National Historical Park's visitor center, which offers exhibits on local history, including the Lewis and Clark Expedition and the Nez Perce War. The town of Orofino (46°29′8″N 116°15′32″W) is another important historical site along the Clearwater River. Originally established during the gold rush of the 1860s, it became a central hub for mining and logging. The Clearwater Historical Museum in Orofino provides a comprehensive look at the area's history, including exhibits on Native American culture, early settlers, and the development of the logging and mining industries.

The construction of the Dworshak Dam (46°30′54″N 116°17′46″W) in the early 1970s significantly impacted the region. The dam, located on the North Fork of the Clearwater River, created the Dworshak Reservoir, which is used for hydroelectric power, flood control, and recreation. Spaulding (46°26′47″N 116°49′06″W) is a historic district named after missionary Henry Harmon Spalding, which includes the site of his mission and farm. Spalding introduced irrigation, schooling, and agricultural practices to the Nez Perce, and his mission was a center of cultural exchange and conflict.

Dworshak Reservoir

Chapter 8: Sawtooth Scenic Byway

20 - State Highway 75: Shoshone to Stanley

Traveling from Shoshone (42°56'12"N 114°24'28"W) to Stanley (44°13'0"N 114°56'16"W) is a picturesque journey that show-cases the natural beauty and diverse landscapes of central Idaho. The 150-mile route primarily follows State Highway 75, offering a mix of scenic views, historical sites, and outdoor recreation opportunities. Shoshone is a small town in Lincoln County known for its rich railroad history and proximity to the Shoshone Ice Caves. The town serves as a gateway to the scenic wonders of central Idaho.

Shoshone to Hailey passes through the scenic Magic Valley with small towns that provide opportunities to explore local shops, restaurants, and historical sites. Hailey is known for its vibrant arts scene and annual events. Hailey to Ketchum is a short drive away from Sun Valley Resort. The Ernest Hemingway Memorial in Ketchum honors the author, who spent considerable time there. Ketchum to Stanley passes through the Sawtooth National Forest to Sanely, a small town renowned for its access to outdoor activities such as rafting, fishing, hiking, and camping. The town serves as a base for exploring the

Sawtooth Wilderness and the Salmon River.

Salmon River

BONUS #3: Stanley Basin

The Stanley Basin (44°13′0″N 114°56′16″W) is a picturesque and ecologically rich area in central Idaho within the Sawtooth National Recreation Area (SNRA). Sitting at about 6,300 feet, it is surrounded by the rugged Sawtooth Mountains, which feature some of the most dramatic and scenic landscapes in the western United States. The Stanley Basin is a broad, glacial valley characterized by expansive meadows, dense forests, and numerous alpine lakes and streams. The Salmon River, known as the "River of No Return," originates here, flowing northward and providing critical habitat for various wildlife species, including salmon and steelhead trout. The basin's terrain is shaped by its glacial history, with moraines, outwash plains, and U-shaped valleys evident throughout the area.

Stanley

The Stanley Basin is a hub for outdoor recreation, drawing visitors year-round. Summer hiking, camping, fishing, kayaking, and mountain biking are popular. Within the SNRA, the Sawtooth Wilderness offers over 700 miles of trails, providing access to pristine alpine environments. The basin becomes a playground for cross-country skiing, snowshoeing, and snowmobiling in winter. The small town of Stanley, located within the basin, serves as the gateway to the Sawtooth Mountains and the SNRA. Despite its small population, Stanley offers essential services and amenities for visitors, including lodging, dining, and outfitter services. The town is known for its friendly atmosphere and serves as a base for exploring the surrounding wilderness.

21 – Sawtooth Highlights: Sun Valley & Galena Summit

Sun Valley (43°40'50"N 114°20'34"W) is a resort city near Ketchum. Nestled in the Rocky Mountains, it is renowned for its exceptional skiing, stunning landscapes, and luxurious amenities. Sun Valley was established in 1936 as America's first destination ski resort by W. Averell Harriman, chairman of the Union Pacific Railroad. The resort was designed to attract wealthy tourists and has since become a premier destination for winter sports. Sun Valley boasts two major ski areas, Bald Mountain (known as Baldy) and Dollar Mountain, offering a variety of terrains for skiers and snowboarders of all levels. Visitors can enjoy hiking, mountain biking, golf, and fly fishing in the warmer months. The area is also famous for its scenic trails and outdoor concerts.

Galena Summit (43°52'12"N 114°42'47"W) is a high mountain pass located in the Sawtooth National Recreation Area. At an elevation of 8,701 feet, it offers breathtaking views and serves as a gateway to the Sawtooth Wilderness. Galena Summit is historically significant as part of the old Galena Road, which was used during the mining boom in the late 19th century. The summit provides a panoramic view of the Sawtooth Range, the Boulder Mountains, and the headwaters of the Salmon River. The lookout point at Galena Summit is one of the most photographed spots in Idaho, offering stunning vistas of alpine meadows, forests, and rugged peaks.

Galena Summit

Chapter 9: Oregon Trail Backcountry Byway

22 - Glenns Ferry to Montpelier

The journey from Glenns Ferry (42°57′7″N 115°18′4″W) to Montpelier (42°19′13″N 111°18′13″W) along the Oregon Trail Backcountry Byway is a captivating route that offers a deep dive into the historical and natural beauty of the American West. This segment of the Oregon Trail, a critical pathway for pioneers heading to the western United States in the 19th century, is rich with historical significance and scenic landscapes. Glenns Ferry was a crucial crossing point on the Snake River for Oregon Trail pioneers. The Three Island Crossing State Park in Glenns Ferry commemorates this historic crossing, offering visitors interpretive trails, exhibits, and reenactments that illustrate the challenges faced by the pioneers.

Several interpretive centers and historical sites offer insights into the pioneer experience throughout the journey, including Massacre Rocks State Park and the Fort Hall Replica. As the trail approaches Montpelier, travelers are treated to the picturesque landscapes of southeastern Idaho. This region is characterized by its rolling hills, lush valleys, and clear streams, including

Bear Lake on the Idaho–Utah border. Traveling the Oregon Trail Backcountry Byway from Glenns Ferry to Montpelier is not just a drive through scenic landscapes; it's a journey through time. The route provides a profound connection to the hardships, triumphs, and everyday lives of the pioneers who traversed these lands over a century ago.

Snake River

23 - Historical Landmarks & Scenic Vistas

The Oregon Trail Backcountry Byway is a captivating route that offers travelers a glimpse into the historic journey of pioneers who traveled westward in the 19th century. This byway, stretching through the picturesque landscapes of Idaho and

Oregon, is replete with historical landmarks and scenic vistas that reflect the region's rich cultural heritage and natural beauty. Three Island Crossing State Park (42°56′41″N 115°19′05″W) marks one of the most significant river crossings along the Oregon Trail. Pioneers had to make a critical decision: cross the treacherous Snake River or take a longer, safer route.

Craters of the Moon National Monument & Preserve

Craters of the Moon National Monument and Preserve (43°27′42″N 113°33′46″W) is an otherworldly landscape created by ancient volcanic activity that offers dramatic vistas of lava fields, cinder cones, and sagebrush. The scenic loop drive provides access to trails, caves, and viewpoints, offering a glimpse into the geological forces that shaped the region. Bruneau Dunes State Park (42°54′36″N 115°42′35″W) is home to the tallest single-structured sand dune in North America. Bruneau Dunes offers a unique and stunning landscape. The park features hiking trails, a small observatory, and expansive views of the surrounding desert and dunes, making it an excellent spot for stargazing and photography. Get more details on these parks in Chapter 11.

Chapter 10: Historical Sites

24 - Idaho City: Gold Rush History

Idaho City (43°49′43″N 115°49′56″W), located in the mountainous region about 36 miles northeast of Boise, has a rich history tied to the Gold Rush era of the mid-19th century. The gold rush in the Boise Basin, which includes Idaho City, started in earnest in 1862. George Grimes and Moses Splawn first discovered gold along Grimes Creek. News of this discovery spread rapidly, and by 1863, thousands of miners had flocked to the region, hoping to strike it rich. This influx of people led to the rapid establishment of mining camps and towns, including Idaho City, which quickly became the largest. During its peak in the 1860s, Idaho City was one of the largest cities in the Northwest. By 1864, the population had swelled to over 7,000, making it the largest city in the Northwest, even larger than Portland, Oregon, at the time. The town thrived with businesses, saloons, and entertainment venues catering to the miners and other settlers.

By the late 1860s, the easily accessible gold had largely been extracted, and the population of Idaho City began to decline as miners moved on to other strikes or returned home. However, the town did not disappear completely. It transformed into a service center for the remaining mining operations in the region. Today, Idaho City is a living museum of the Gold Rush era. Its historic buildings have been preserved or restored, offering a glimpse into the past. The city is a popular destination for tourists interested in gold rush history and outdoor activities in the surrounding Boise National Forest.

Idaho City

25 - Old Idaho Penitentiary: Prison History Tour

The Old Idaho Penitentiary (43.6027°N 116.162°W) is a historical site that offers a fascinating glimpse into the state's past through its Prison History Tour. This tour provides visitors with an in-depth look at the history and operations of the prison, which was in use from 1872 to 1973. The Old Idaho Penitentiary features several historic buildings, including cell blocks, solitary confinement cells, and the gallows. Each structure has been preserved to maintain its historical integrity, allowing visitors to step back in time and experience the inmates' conditions. The Old Idaho Penitentiary housed some of Idaho's most infamous criminals. The tour often highlights the stories of these notorious inmates, providing insight into their crimes, lives, and impact on the penitentiary's history.

Old Idaho Penitentiary

Visitors to the Old Idaho Penitentiary can expect a unique and educational experience. The tour provides a sobering look at the realities of historical incarceration, emphasizing the changes in the penal system over the last century. It's an opportunity to learn about the social, political, and legal aspects of Idaho's history in a tangible and impactful way. Whether you're a history enthusiast, interested in criminal justice, or simply looking for an intriguing outing, the Prison History Tour at the Old Idaho Penitentiary offers a compelling and thought-provoking journey through the past.

Chapter 11: Geological Wonders

26 - Craters of the Moon

Craters of the Moon National Monument and Preserve (43°27′42″N 113°33′46″W) is a unique and otherworldly landscape that spans approximately 750,000 acres and features extensive volcanic fields. The monument is named for its striking resemblance to the lunar surface, with its rugged terrain, dark basalt rock, and numerous volcanic craters and cones. The Craters of the Moon region is part of the Snake River Plain, which has experienced volcanic activity over the past 15 million years. The most recent eruptions occurred between 2,100 and 15,000 years ago, making it a relatively young volcanic field. The area consists of three major lava fields—Great Rift, Kings Bowl, and Wapi—containing some of the best-preserved basaltic lava flows in the continental United States.

Craters of the Moon offers a variety of recreational activities for visitors. Popular activities include hiking, trails ranging from easy walks to more challenging backcountry routes, caving in the numerous lava tubes, and camping. The scenic Loop Road provides access to many of the key features, and ranger-led programs offer educational insights into the geology and ecology of the area. Winter transforms the landscape, providing opportunities for snowshoeing and cross-country skiing. The stark, snow-covered terrain adds another layer of beauty to this stunning landscape.

Craters of the Moon National Monument & Preserve

27 - Balanced Rock

Balanced Rock is a striking natural formation in Salmon Falls Creek Canyon near Buhl (42°36′0″N 114°45′43″W) in the Magic Valley region. This geological marvel is renowned for its precarious appearance and impressive size. Balanced Rock stands approximately 48 feet (14.6 meters) tall and weighs around 40 tons. Its unique shape features a narrow base about 3 feet (0.9

meters) in diameter. It supports a much larger top, making it look delicately balanced, and can topple over any moment. The rock's unusual shape was formed through centuries of natural weathering and erosion, which sculpted it from the surrounding softer rock.

Balanced Rock is situated in Balanced Rock Park, a small but charming park managed by Twin Falls County. The park is accessible via a short drive from Buhl, making it a popular destination for locals and tourists. Visitors can park nearby and take a short hike to get a closer view of the rock and enjoy the surrounding natural beauty. The rock is a popular spot for photography, given its dramatic appearance and the stunning backdrop of the Magic Valley.

28 - Bruneau Dunes

Bruneau Dunes State Park (42°54′36″N 115°42′35″W) boasts the tallest single-structured sand dune in North America. The dunes rise nearly 470 feet above the surrounding desert floor, making them a striking feature in the otherwise flat landscape. This remarkable state park covers approximately 4,800 acres and offers a variety of recreational opportunities for visitors. The Bruneau Dunes were formed over thousands of years by wind action. The sand that composes the dunes is believed to have originated from the Bonneville Flood, a prehistoric event that dramatically reshaped the landscape of the Pacific Northwest. Over time, prevailing winds from the west and southwest carried sand particles to the area, accumulating to form the dunes we see today.

Bruneau Dunes State Park is a popular destination for outdoor enthusiasts. Visitors can hike to the top of the dunes for a panoramic view of the surrounding area. Sandboarding, similar to snowboarding but on sand, is a thrilling activity that attracts many adventurers. Bruneau Dunes is known for its clear night skies, making it a fantastic location for stargazing. The park even has its own observatory, which hosts public viewing nights and astronomy programs. The park features two small lakes where visitors can fish for bluegill, bass, and catfish. Non-motorized boats are allowed, making it a peaceful spot for kayaking and canoeing. The park offers several camping options, including serviced campsites, primitive sites, and cabins. This makes it an ideal place to explore the area for a weekend getaway or an extended stay.

Bruneau Dunes State Park

Chapter 12: Wildlife Viewing

29 – Birdwatching at Deer Flat National Wildlife Refuge

Deer Flat National Wildlife Refuge (43°33′N 116°40′W) includes wetlands, riparian areas, sagebrush steppe, and agricultural lands, each supporting different bird populations. This habitat diversity makes the refuge a critical stopover for migratory birds on the Pacific Flyway and a haven for resident species. Bird watching at Deer Flat National Wildlife Refuge is a captivating experience for both novice and experienced birders. The refuge encompasses Lake Lowell and surrounding lands, offering diverse habitats that attract various bird species.

Lake Lowell, the centerpiece of the refuge, provides excellent opportunities to observe waterfowl. In the winter, large flocks of ducks, geese, and swans can be seen on the lake. Species such as the Northern Pintail, Mallard, and Tundra Swan are commonly spotted. The shoreline and adjacent wetlands are perfect for spotting wading birds like the Great Blue Heron and American Avocet. During spring and fall migration, the refuge comes alive with migratory birds. Warblers, flycatchers, and shorebirds are abundant, making it an ideal time for bird watchers to visit. The sight of thousands of Snow Geese taking flight is a spectacular highlight. Several observation blinds and platforms are strategically placed around the refuge, offering discreet viewing spots to minimize disturbance to the wildlife.

Lake Lowell

30 – Moose and Elk Spotting in the Selkirk Mountains

Moose and elk spotting in the Selkirk Mountains is a captivating experience for wildlife enthusiasts and nature lovers. The Selkirk Mountains, extending into northern Idaho, northeastern Washington, and southeastern British Columbia, are characterized by their rugged terrain, dense forests, alpine meadows, and crystal-clear lakes. This diverse landscape provides ideal habitats for a wide range of wildlife, including the majestic moose and elk.

Selkirk Mountains

Moose thrive in the wetland areas of the Selkirk Mountains. They are often found near lakes, rivers, and marshy regions, feeding on aquatic vegetation, willows, and other shrubs. Moose are solitary animals, except during mating season in the fall. Priest Lake (48°34′N 116°52′W) is known for frequent moose sightings, especially around the shoreline and wetlands. Elk are social animals often found in herds. They prefer open forests, meadows, and valleys where they graze on grasses, plants, and tree bark. During the fall rutting season, male elk (bulls) can be heard bugling, a distinctive call to attract females and establish dominance. Selkirk Crest (48.8455°N 116.5544°W) and other higher-elevation open meadows are ideal for spotting elk. The Kaniksu National Forest (48.317°N 116.152°W) combines dense forest and open spaces, perfect for elk sightings.

31 – Seasonal Migrations in the Camas National Wildlife Refuge

Watching seasonal migrations in the Camas National Wildlife Refuge (43.95129°N 112.24914°W) is a spectacular experience that offers a front-row seat to one of nature's most remarkable phenomena. Located in eastern Idaho, the refuge spans over 10,578 acres and provides critical habitat for various migratory birds and other wildlife. In the spring, the refuge comes alive with the arrival of migratory birds returning from their wintering grounds. This period, typically from March to May, sees an influx of waterfowl, shorebirds, and songbirds. Among the most notable are the sandhill cranes, whose distinctive calls and graceful flight patterns are a highlight for bird watchers. Ducks, geese, and swans also appear prominent, utilizing the refuge's wetlands for resting and feeding. The vibrant display of breeding plumage and the energetic courtship behaviors add to the excitement of spring birding.

Autumn is another prime time for observing migrations from September to November. As the birds prepare for their journey to warmer climates, the refuge becomes a bustling hub of activity. Large flocks of waterfowl gather, including pintails, mallards, and teal. Raptors such as bald eagles and northern harriers can be seen hunting over the fields and wetlands. A sense of urgency marks the fall migration as birds stock up on food to fuel their long flights.

Camas Prairie

Chapter 13: Cultural Experiences

32 – The Basque Block in Boise

The Basque Block in Boise, Idaho, is a vibrant cultural enclave that celebrates the rich heritage of the Basque people. Originally from the region spanning the border between Spain and France, this unique area is located on Grove Street in downtown Boise and serves as a focal point for the Basque community. The Basque Block's origins date back to the late 19th and early 20th centuries when many Basques emigrated to the United States, with a significant number settling in Idaho.

The Basque Museum and Cultural Center is the cornerstone of the Basque Block. It offers exhibits that delve into the Basque people's history, culture, and contributions in Idaho and beyond. The Basque Market, known for its authentic Basque cuisine, this market provides a taste of traditional dishes such as paella, pintxos (Basque tapas), and chorizo. The Historic Cyrus Jacobs-Uberuaga House was built in 1864 and later became a boarding house for Basque immigrants. It is one of the oldest surviving buildings in Boise and offers a glimpse into the early lives of Basque settlers. Bar Gernika is a popular spot for both locals and visitors. This bar serves traditional Basque food and drinks, providing a casual and friendly atmosphere in which to enjoy the Basque Block's cultural ambiance.

Basque Block, Boise

33 - Sun Valley Film Festival (SVFF)

The Sun Valley Film Festival (43°40'50"N 114°20'34"W) is a celebrated annual event held in Sun Valley, Idaho, known for its scenic beauty and rich cultural offerings. Since its inception in 2012, the festival has become a significant platform for independent filmmakers, attracting industry professionals, enthusiasts, and media. SVFF showcases a wide range of films, including feature films, documentaries, and short films. The festival prides itself on presenting established and emerging filmmakers, offering audiences a unique blend of cinematic experiences.

The festival hosts various forums and panels where filmmakers, actors, producers, and other industry experts discuss trends, challenges, and innovations in the film industry. Reflecting Sun Valley's reputation as an outdoor haven, the festival often includes films and discussions about adventure, the environment, and the great outdoors, resonating with the local community's love for nature. The festival has drawn high-profile attendees, including well-known actors, directors, and producers.

Sun Valley

Chapter 14: Waterfalls

34 - Perrine Coulee Falls

Perrine Coulee Falls (42°35′5″N 114°28′21″W) near Twin Falls is a remarkable location for both BASE jumping and photography. The convergence of natural beauty and extreme sports creates an exciting and visually captivating experience. Whether you're a thrill-seeker looking to leap into the void or a photographer aiming to capture the perfect shot, Perrine Coulee Falls offers an unparalleled setting for adventure and artistry. The falls drop 200 feet, providing an adrenaline-pumping descent with a stunning natural backdrop. BASE jumpers at Perrine Coulee Falls experience a unique combination of freefall and scenery. The jump starts with a leap from a designated platform near the top of the falls. As they descend, jumpers are surrounded by the thunderous roar of the falls and the mist created by the cascading water. The Perrine Bridge, another popular BASE jumping site nearby, adds to the locale's reputation for adventure sports.

Perrine Coulee Falls is a picturesque location, making it a favorite among photographers. The falls' 200-foot drop creates a dramatic scene ideal for photographers. The best time to capture the falls is during the golden hours when the lighting is soft and warm, enhancing the area's natural beauty.[1]

Perrine Bridge, Twin Falls

35 - Mesa Falls

Mesa Falls is situated along the Henrys Fork of the Snake River in the Caribou-Targhee National Forest. The falls are accessible via the Mesa Falls Scenic Byway, a picturesque route that offers breathtaking views of the surrounding wilderness.

---

[1] Safety is paramount in BASE jumping. Jumpers must wear appropriate gear, including a parachute rig designed for BASE jumps, a helmet, and often a wingsuit for more experienced jumpers. Proper training and familiarity with the site conditions, such as wind speed and direction, are essential to ensure a safe jump.

This byway connects the towns of Ashton and Island Park and is easily reachable from larger cities like Idaho Falls and West Yellowstone. Mesa Falls comprises two stunning waterfalls, the Upper and Lower Mesa Falls. This destination is a must-visit for nature enthusiasts and adventure seekers.

Upper Mesa Falls

Upper Mesa Falls (44°11′5″N 111°19′48″W) is the larger of the two, with a drop of about 114 feet and a width of 200 feet. Visitors can enjoy a close-up view from a well-maintained boardwalk and viewing platforms, which provide spectacular vantage points. The thundering sound of the water and the mist rising from the falls create a mesmerizing and immersive experience. Lower Mesa Falls (44°10′5″N 111°19′11″W), though slightly smaller, is equally impressive. With a drop of around 85 feet, it can be viewed from various points along the trails that meander through the area. While there is not as direct access to the base of Lower Mesa Falls as there is for Upper Mesa Falls, the views from the surrounding areas offer a beautiful perspective of the cascading waters.

36 - Rock Climbing and Photography at Twin Falls

Twin Falls (42°35′5″N 114°21′14″W) offers a diverse range of rock climbing opportunities that cater to novice and experienced climbers. The region is characterized by its stunning Snake River Canyon, towering basalt cliffs, and unique rock formations. The picturesque landscape and climbing routes make Twin Falls popular for outdoor enthusiasts. Dierkes Lake offers both bouldering and sport climbing routes. There are numerous bolted routes ranging from 5.6 to 5.12 in difficulty, making it suitable for climbers of various skill levels.

Pillar Falls, with its pillar-like rock formations, provides unique climbing experiences. Auger Falls offers a mix of sport and traditional climbing routes, with impressive views of the Snake River Canyon. Twin Falls is a haven for photographers, offering breathtaking landscapes and dynamic natural features. The canyon's interplay of light and shadow and striking basalt formations provides endless opportunities for stunning shots.

Dierkes Lake

Chapter 15: Hot Springs

37 - Kirkham Hot Springs

Kirkham Hot Springs (44.081°N 115.616°W) is a popular natural hot spring near Lowman in the Boise National Forest. Renowned for its picturesque setting and relaxing thermal pools, it offers visitors a unique and rejuvenating outdoor experience. Kirkham Hot Springs is situated along the South Fork of the Payette River, approximately four miles east of Lowman on State Highway 21. This scenic route, often called the "Ponderosa Pine Scenic Byway," provides stunning views of forested mountains and river landscapes. The hot springs are easily accessible, with a parking area and a short trail leading down to the springs.

Kirkham Hot Springs

The hot springs feature multiple soaking pools of varying temperatures, ranging from warm to hot, allowing visitors to find a spot that suits their comfort level. The pools are fed by natural geothermal water that seeps from the rocks and cascades down in small waterfalls, creating a serene and natural spa-like environment. Kirkham Hot Springs can be enjoyed year-round, offering a different experience each season.

38 - Goldbug Hot Springs

Goldbug Hot Springs (44.905°N 113.929°W) is a scenic and secluded natural hot spring in the Salmon-Challis National Forest near Salmon. It offers visitors a unique opportunity to soak in natural hot springs while enjoying breathtaking views of the surrounding wilderness. Goldbug Hot Springs is situated about 23 miles south of Salmon, Idaho. To reach the springs, visitors must embark on a moderately challenging hike. The trailhead is near mile marker 282 on Highway 93, with a small parking area. The hike to the hot springs is approximately two miles each way, with an elevation gain of around 1,350 feet. The trail winds through a picturesque canyon, crossing small creeks and climbing over rocky terrain. Hikers are rewarded with stunning views along the way.

Goldbug Hot Springs

The hot springs consist of pools cascading down the mountainside, fed by hot water seeping from the rocks. The water temperature varies from pool to pool, allowing visitors to choose a spot that suits their comfort level. The upper pools are the hottest, with temperatures cooling slightly as the water flows downstream. The natural rock formations create a series of inviting pools, perfect for relaxing amidst the rugged beauty of Idaho's wilderness.

39 - Burgdorf Hot Springs

Burgdorf Hot Springs (45.277°N 115.914°W) is a historic and rustic resort located in the mountains of central Idaho, about 30 miles north of McCall. Nestled in the Payette National Forest, these natural hot springs destinations offer a unique and tranquil retreat. It was initially established as a mining camp in the 1860s, during the gold rush era. Miners discovered the hot springs using the naturally heated mineral waters to relax and rejuvenate. The resort was officially founded in 1870 by Fred C. Burgdorf, who saw the potential for a healing retreat in the area.

The resort features a large, open-air hot pool fed by natural geothermal springs. The water, rich in minerals, maintains a temperature of approximately 113°F (45°C) at the source and is cooled to a comfortable level in the soaking pools. The main pool is spacious, allowing plenty of room for guests to spread out and enjoy the soothing waters. Additionally, there are two smaller, hotter pools for those who prefer a more intense soaking experience. Staying at Burgdorf Hot Springs is a unique experience, as it offers rustic accommodations that enhance the feeling of stepping back in time. The resort features a collection of historic log cabins, some dating back to the early 20th century.

Burgdorf Hot Springs

BONUS #4: Heise Hot Springs

Heise Hot Springs (43°37′48″N 111°46′23″W) near Ririe is a popular destination known for its natural mineral hot springs, recreational activities, and stunning surroundings. The hot springs have been a treasured site for relaxation and enjoyment since the late 19th century. Heise Hot Springs was established in 1891 by James Heise, who recognized the potential of the natural hot springs on his land. Over the years, the area has developed into a well-loved retreat, attracting visitors seeking the therapeutic benefits of the mineral-rich waters. The hot pool is filled with naturally heated mineral water, providing a soothing and relaxing experience. The high mineral content is believed to offer various health benefits, such as improved circulation and relief from muscle aches. The warm pool is slightly cooler than the hot pool, ideal for those who prefer a milder temperature while enjoying the mineral water's benefits. The swimming pool is a larger one that is perfect for families and recreational swimming. It's open during the warmer months and features a water slide for added fun.

Various accommodation options, including RV camping, tent sites, and cabins, make it convenient for day-trippers and overnight guests. The property features a picturesque nine-hole golf course, providing a leisurely activity amidst the beautiful Idaho landscape. For adventure enthusiasts, the zip line offers an exhilarating way to take in the views of the surrounding area. The location of Heise Hot Springs provides easy access to various outdoor activities. Visitors can enjoy hiking, fishing, and wildlife viewing nearby. The proximity to the Snake River adds opportunities for river activities like tubing and kayaking.

BONUS #5: Big (Cold) Springs

Big Springs (44°30'01"N 111°15'19"W) is a significant and picturesque natural feature located in Island Park. This unique site is renowned for being one of the largest natural springs in the world, and it serves as the primary source of the Henrys Fork of the Snake River. Big Springs is notable for its impressive discharge of clear, cold water. It produces over 120 million gallons of water daily, fed by snowmelt and underground aquifers. The water maintains a constant temperature of around 52 degrees Fahrenheit throughout the year.

Big Springs Cabins

The ecosystem around Big Springs is rich and diverse, providing a habitat for various wildlife species. The area is mainly known for its population of large rainbow trout, which can be seen swimming in the spring's clear waters. Fishing is not allowed in the spring to protect this natural habitat, but the surrounding areas offer ample opportunities for anglers. The gentle flow of the Henrys Fork near Big Springs is ideal for canoeing and kayaking activities, offering a serene way to explore the area's natural beauty. Several trails in the vicinity provide opportunities for hiking and exploring the lush forests and meadows. The diverse fauna and flora make Big Springs a prime location for observing wildlife in their natural habitats.

Chapter 16: Caves and Canyons

40 - Mammoth Cave

Mammoth Cave is a lava tube formed by volcanic activity approximately 30,000 years ago. As surface lava cooled and solidified, the molten lava beneath continued to flow, eventually emptying and leaving a hollow tube. This process created the extensive underground passageways that characterize Mammoth Cave. The cave stretches over a quarter of a mile and offers a cool, stable climate year-round, making it a comfortable exploration site even during hot summer. Visitors can observe the smooth walls and floors typical of lava tubes and various formations, such as stalactites and stalagmites formed by the slow deposition of minerals over millennia.

Mammoth Cave is open to the public and can be explored through guided tours. These tours provide insights into the cave's geological history, formation processes, and the types of lava and rock formations present. Visitors often appreciate the chance to experience the cave's natural beauty and tranquil, otherworldly atmosphere. In addition to Mammoth Cave, the surrounding area offers other attractions, such as the Shoshone Ice Caves, another set of lava tubes that maintain icy temperatures even in summer. The region is rich in geological history and provides opportunities for hiking, viewing wildlife, and exploring southern Idaho's high desert landscape.

Shoshone Ice Cave

41 - Box Canyon

Box Canyon (42°51′28″N 114°52′35″W) is a stunning geological feature renowned for its dramatic scenery and unique natural attributes. Situated near Wendell in the Hagerman Valley, this canyon is part of the more extensive Snake River Plain, a region marked by volcanic activity and the meandering Snake River. Box Canyon is primarily known for its impressive cliffs and clear, blue-green waters. The canyon was formed through a combination of volcanic activity and subsequent erosion by water. The Snake River Plain results from volcanic eruptions that occurred millions of years ago, and the basaltic lava flows laid the groundwork for the landscape today. Over time, water from springs and the river has carved out deep canyons, with Box Canyon being one of the most notable examples.

The canyon's walls rise dramatically, creating a secluded and serene environment. Hiking trails along the rim offer breathtaking views of the canyon and the surrounding landscape. For those looking to explore further, paths descend into the canyon, allowing for closer inspection of the water features and rock formations.

Box Canyon

42 - Malad Gorge

Malad Gorge (42°51′28″N 114°52′35″W) is a striking natural feature within the Thousand Springs State Park. Known for its dramatic landscapes, the gorge is carved by the Malad River, which flows through it, creating a scenic and rugged canyon approximately 250 feet deep and 2.5 miles long. The gorge offers a remarkable view of geological formations and attracts visitors interested in natural history, geology, and outdoor activities. Malad Gorge showcases impressive basalt rock formations resulting from ancient volcanic activity. The canyon's walls, composed primarily of basalt, provide a glimpse into the region's volcanic past. The gorge was formed by the Malad River cutting through these basalt layers, creating a steep and narrow canyon that continues to evolve due to erosion and other geological processes.

One of the highlights of Malad Gorge is its series of waterfalls and springs. The most prominent waterfall is "Devil's Washbowl," where the Malad River cascades into the gorge, creating a powerful and picturesque waterfall. The Thousand Springs, part of the Snake River Aquifer, contribute to the river's flow, emerging from the canyon walls and adding to the area's lushness and beauty. The state park offers several amenities, including hiking trails, picnic areas, and viewpoints that provide stunning vistas of the gorge and its waterfalls. The interpretive trails and signs help visitors learn about the geological and ecological significance of the area. Additionally, the park's proximity to Interstate 84 makes it an easily accessible stop for travelers exploring southern Idaho.

Malad Gorge

Chapter 17: Theme Parks and Zoos

43 – Zoo Idaho

Zoo Idaho (42.8427°N 112.4218°W) in Pocatello offers a unique and enriching experience focused on the conservation and education of native wildlife. Established in 1932, the zoo spans over 25 acres within the confines of the scenic Ross Park, providing a naturalistic habitat for its animal residents and a serene environment for visitors. The zoo is home to a diverse range of species, all indigenous to the region. The American Bison are iconic creatures that symbolize the American West's wildlife heritage. Grizzly Bears, powerful and awe-inspiring, these bears highlight the importance of habitat preservation. Bald Eagles, representing American wildlife's strength and freedom, are a favorite among visitors.

A visit to Zoo Idaho promises a memorable and educational adventure. The scenic setting and well-designed exhibits allow for a leisurely and immersive experience. Picnic areas, walking trails, and playgrounds make it family friendly. The zoo's gift shop offers souvenirs that support its conservation efforts, allowing visitors to take a piece of their experience home.

44 - Silverwood Theme Park

Silverwood Theme Park (47.9085°N 116.705°W) in Athol is the largest theme park in the Pacific Northwest. Opened in 1988 by Gary Norton, the park has grown significantly from its humble beginnings and now spans over 413 acres, offering various attractions and entertainment options. Silverwood includes several roller coasters (Aftershock, Corkscrew, Timber Terror, Tremors, Stunt Pilot) and various rides suitable for families, including the antique car ride, Ferris wheel, and log flume. These attractions provide a more relaxed and enjoyable experience for visitors of all ages.

Timber Terror

Boulder Beach is a major highlight of Silverwood. It features numerous water slides, wave pools, and a lazy river. Silverwood hosts various events throughout the year, including seasonal celebrations like Scarywood during Halloween, where the park is transformed with haunted attractions and spooky entertainment. The park also features live shows, including magic shows and musical performances catering to a broad audience. With its blend of thrilling rides, family-friendly attractions, and water park fun, Silverwood provides a well-rounded experience for visitors. The park's scenic setting in northern Idaho adds to its charm, offering beautiful views and a pleasant atmosphere.

Chapter 18: Educational Centers

45 - Discovery Center of Idaho

Discovery Center of Idaho (dcidaho.org), located in Boise, is a premier interactive science museum dedicated to inspiring lifelong interest and learning in science, technology, engineering, and mathematics (STEM). Established in 1988, the center aims to provide hands-on educational experiences for visitors of all ages. It is housed in a spacious facility in downtown Boise, providing ample room for exhibits and activities. It includes amenities such as a gift shop offering educational toys, science kits, and a café for visitors to relax.

The Discovery Center of Idaho features various exhibits covering a broad spectrum of scientific disciplines. These exhibits are designed to be interactive, encouraging visitors to engage directly with the demonstrated scientific principles. Permanent exhibits feature various topics from physics and engineering to biology and environmental science. They are designed to be engaging and educational, offering hands-on experiences that make learning fun and memorable. Temporary exhibits cover specific themes or topics, often collaborating with other museums and scientific institutions. These exhibits ensure that there is always something new to explore, keeping the experience fresh for repeat visitors.

Inside Discovery Center of Idaho

46 - Idaho Museum of Natural History

The Idaho Museum of Natural History (isu.edu/imnh) is located on the campus of Idaho State University in Pocatello. It is a significant cultural and educational resource focusing on Idaho's natural history, cultural heritage, and the Intermountain West. The museum boasts extensive collections that span various fields, including paleontology, anthropology, archaeology, earth sciences, and life sciences. Its exhibits are designed to engage a diverse audience, from school children to researchers and general visitors. Key exhibits often feature dinosaur fossils, including species unique to the region, as well as artifacts from ancient Native American cultures, providing insights into the historical inhabitants of Idaho.

The Idaho Museum of Natural History strongly emphasizes community engagement. It regularly hosts events such as lectures, family days, and special exhibitions that attract regional visitors. These events are designed to be both educational and entertaining, fostering a deeper appreciation for natural history and cultural heritage. The museum also offers volunteer opportunities, allowing community members to participate and support its mission. The Idaho Museum of Natural History is more than just a repository of artifacts; it is a dynamic institution dedicated to education, research, and community engagement.

47 - World Center for Birds of Prey

The World Center for Birds of Prey (peregrinefund.org/visit) in Boise is a premier facility dedicated to the conservation, education, and research of birds of prey, also known as raptors. Established by The Peregrine Fund in 1984, the center plays a pivotal role in preserving various raptor species. The Center has an interpretive center featuring interactive exhibits that provide insights into raptors' life cycles, habitats, and conservation needs. Highlights include the Archives of Falconry, which showcases the art and history of falconry. Outdoor flight displays allow visitors to witness live raptor demonstrations, showcasing the hunting techniques and flight capabilities of birds such as falcons, hawks, and eagles. Specialized breeding enclosures support the propagation of endangered species, contributing to reintroducing raptors into the wild.

Chapter 19: Festivals and Fairs

48 - Western Idaho Fair

The Western Idaho Fair is an annual event held in Boise, typically in August. This fair has a long-standing tradition dating back to 1897, making it one of the region's most beloved and enduring events. The fair celebrates the local agricultural community, offering various activities, competitions, and entertainment for all ages. A central feature of the Western Idaho Fair is its extensive exhibitions and competitions. These include livestock shows, where farmers compete for top honors with their cattle, pigs, sheep, and other animals. There are also horticultural displays, home arts, and crafts competitions, and contests for baked goods, preserves, and other homemade products. These competitions highlight the skills and dedication of the participants and offer a glimpse into the rich agricultural traditions of Idaho.

The fair is known for its vibrant and diverse entertainment options. Visitors can enjoy carnival rides, games, and a variety of live performances. Music is a major draw, with concerts featuring local talent and nationally known artists spanning multiple genres. Additionally, the fair hosts a rodeo, demolition derby, and various motorsports events, providing high-energy entertainment for thrill-seekers. Food is a highlight of the Western Idaho Fair, with a wide selection of vendors offering everything from traditional fair favorites like corn dogs, funnel cakes, and cotton candy to unique local specialties. The fair also features numerous commercial vendors selling various products, from handmade crafts to the latest agricultural technology. The fair is designed to be a family-friendly event, with multiple activities and attractions tailored specifically for children. There are petting zoos, pony rides, and interactive educational exhibits that teach kids about farming and agriculture. The fair's emphasis on family fun makes it a popular destination for parents looking to spend quality time with their children.

Ride at the Western Idaho Fair

49 - Trailing of the Sheep Festival

The Trailing of the Sheep Festival is a unique and vibrant celebration of Idaho's rich sheep ranching heritage and cultural traditions. This festival typically occurs in October in the Wood River Valley, including the towns of Ketchum, Hailey, and Sun Valley. The event draws thousands of visitors from around the world who come to witness and participate in the festivities. The festival honors the long-standing sheepherding tradition in Idaho, which dates back to the late 19th century. Basque, Scottish, and Peruvian immigrants, among others, played a significant role in developing the sheep industry in the region. The festival celebrates sheep's agricultural importance and highlights these immigrant communities' diverse cultural contributions.

Trailing of the Sheep Festival

One of the festival's central attractions is the "Trailing of the Sheep Parade," where hundreds of sheep are herded through the streets of Ketchum. This event vividly reminds us of the seasonal migration, or trailing, of sheep from high mountain summer pastures to lower winter grazing areas. This practice has been part of Idaho's agricultural life for generations. Other activities include sheepdog trials that showcase the skills of highly trained sheepdogs and their handlers as they maneuver sheep through various obstacles. The folklife fair features traditional music, dance, and crafts, providing a platform for cultural expressions related to sheep herding. Attendees can enjoy performances by Basque dancers, Peruvian musicians, and Scottish bagpipers. The wool festival focuses on the art of wool production, with spinning, weaving, and dyeing demonstrations. Artisans show-case and sell their woolen goods, from clothing to home décor.

50 - Art in the Park

Art in the Park is an annual event held in Boise, typically hosted by the Boise Art Museum (BAM). This vibrant arts festival takes place in the picturesque Julia Davis Park (43°36′27.2″N 116°12′5.44″W), offering a unique blend of art, culture, and community spirit. The event has a rich history, having been celebrated for several decades, and it has grown into one of the region's most significant cultural gatherings. Art in the Park features a wide array of artwork from over 200 artists and artisans nationwide. Attendees can explore booths showcasing a variety of mediums, including painting, sculpture, ceramics, jewelry, photography, and mixed media. This diversity allows visitors to appreciate different artistic styles and techniques.

The event encourages community participation through interactive art experiences. Workshops, demonstrations, and hands-on activities are available for attendees of all ages, fostering a deeper appreciation for the creative process. These interactive elements make Art in the Park an exhibition and a participatory celebration of art. Complementing the visual arts, Art in the Park also features live performances from local musicians, dancers, and theater groups. These performances add a dynamic auditory and visual element to the festival, enhancing the overall atmosphere and providing entertainment for all attendees. Various food vendors are present, offering an assortment of culinary delights. From local food trucks to gourmet snacks, the festival offers a range of options to satisfy different tastes. There are also beverage stalls providing alcoholic and non-alcoholic drinks, ensuring a festive and enjoyable experience.

Chapter 20: The Spirit of Idaho

As we reach the end of our journey through Idaho's hidden gems and lesser-known marvels, it's time to reflect on our adventures. From serene landscapes to thrilling escapades, Idaho has proven to be a state brimming with opportunities for exploration and discovery beyond its famed national parks.

Each adventure has its unique story, enriching our understanding and appreciation of this remarkable state. We've traversed mountain trails, delved into mysterious caves, paddled through pristine waters, and strolled through historic towns. Whether a quiet lake or a bustling farmer's market, every location contributes to the vibrant tapestry that makes Idaho unique.

Unveiling Hidden Treasures

One of the most rewarding aspects of our journey has been uncovering Idaho's hidden treasures. Often overshadowed by more famous landmarks, these spots offer a chance to experience the state's natural beauty and cultural richness more intimately and personally. The secluded hot springs, tranquil rivers, and off-the-beaten-path hiking trails have shown us that adventure doesn't always mean venturing far from home; sometimes, it means looking a little closer at what's right in front of us.

Embracing the Spirit of Adventure

Idaho teaches us that adventure comes in many forms. It's about more than just scaling the highest peak or navigating the roughest waters. Sometimes, it's about the quiet moments— watching a sunset over a calm lake, savoring a freshly picked huckleberry, or listening to the sounds of the forest. It's about stepping out of our comfort zones, whether trying a new activity or simply exploring a new part of town.

The adventures we've chronicled in this book are just a starting point. Idaho is vast and varied, with countless more experiences waiting to be discovered. We've highlighted 50 adventures, but there are always new trails to hike, rivers to float, and communities to explore. Each adventure is an invitation to connect with the natural world, to learn something new, and to create lasting memories.

Your Next Adventure

As you close this book, remember that the spirit of adventure lives on in each of us. Idaho's grand and humble landscapes call out to be explored. Whether you're a seasoned adventurer or just starting to discover the joys of outdoor exploration, Idaho offers endless possibilities.

Take the knowledge and inspiration from these pages and

make your own Idaho adventure. Seek new paths, revisit favorite spots, and continue exploring this state's wonders. Every adventure, no matter how small, adds to the rich tapestry of your journey.

THANK YOU!!

Thank you for joining us on this exploration of Idaho's hidden gems. May your future adventures be filled with discovery, joy, and the boundless beauty of Idaho.

Happy trails!

Also by Ford Powell

 **Utah Adventures: 50 Adventures that are not National Parks (plus a few bonuses)**

Made in United States
Troutdale, OR
12/12/2024

26367006R00058